THE COMPLETE PIANO
90s HITS

Arranged by Kenneth Baker

Wise Publications
London/New York/Paris/Sydney/Copenhagen/Madrid

Exclusive Distributors:
Music Sales Limited
8/9 Frith Street,
London W1V 5TZ,
England.
Music Sales Pty Limited
120 Rothschild Avenue,
Rosebery, NSW 2018,
Australia.

This book © Copyright 1998 by Wise Publications
Order No. AM952699
ISBN 0-7119-7161-7

Compiled by Peter Evans
Music arranged by Kenneth Baker
Music processed by MSS Studios

Cover design by Studio Twenty, London
Cover illustration based on original Photographs by
London Features International, M.P.A., Retna Pictures,
Rex Features and Pearce Marchbank

Your Guarantee of Quality
As publishers, we strive to produce every book to the
highest commercial standards.
The music has been freshly engraved and the book has been
carefully designed to minimise awkward page turns and to
make playing from it a real pleasure.
Particular care has been given to specifying acid-free, neutral-sized
paper made from pulps which have not been elemental chlorine bleached.
This pulp is from farmed sustainable forests and was produced with
special regard for the environment.
Throughout, the printing and binding have been planned to ensure a sturdy,
attractive publication which should give years of enjoyment.
If your copy fails to meet our high standards, please
inform us and we will gladly replace it.

Music Sales' complete catalogue describes thousands of titles and is
available in full colour sections by subject, direct from Music Sales Limited.
Please state your areas of interest and send a cheque/postal order for £1.50 for postage to:
Music Sales Limited, Newmarket Road, Bury St. Edmunds, Suffolk IP33 3YB.

Visit the Internet Music Shop at
http://www.musicsales.co.uk

Printed in the Great Britain by
Printwise (Haverhill) Limited, Haverhill, Suffolk.

AS LONG AS YOU LOVE ME

Words & Music by Max Martin

BARBIE GIRL

Words & Music by Soren Rasted, Claus Norreen, Rene Dif, Lene Nystrom,
Johnny Pederson & Karsten Dahlgaard

TOO MUCH

Words & Music by Victoria Aadams, Emma Bunton, Melanie Brown, Melanie Chisholm,
Geri Halliwell, Paul Wilson & Andy Watkins

DON'T YOU LOVE ME

Words & Music by Cynthia Biggs, Carolyn Mitchell, Terence Dudley & Christopher Kellum

Lyrics:
1. Child goes to the store for a loaf of bread, — don't you love me, — don't you love me no more? —

Bul- lets fly- ing all a - round his head, — don't you love me, — don't you

TELL HIM

Words & Music by Linda Thompson, Walter Afanasieff & David Foster

WILD WOOD

Words & Music by Paul Weller

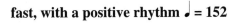

fast, with a positive rhythm ♩ = 152

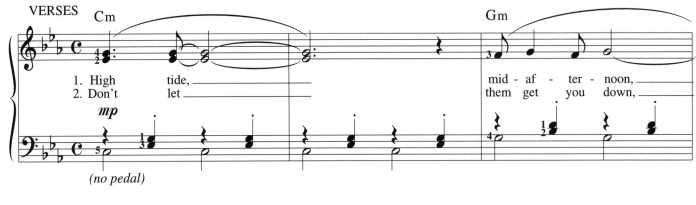

1. High   tide,   mid-af-ter-noon,
2. Don't   let   them get you down,

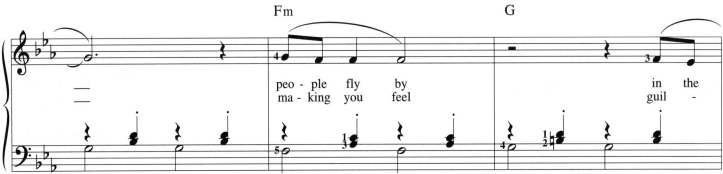

peo-ple fly by   in the
ma-king you feel   guil-

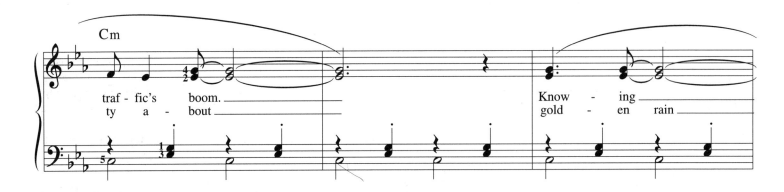

traf-fic's boom.   Know-ing
ty a-bout   gold-en rain

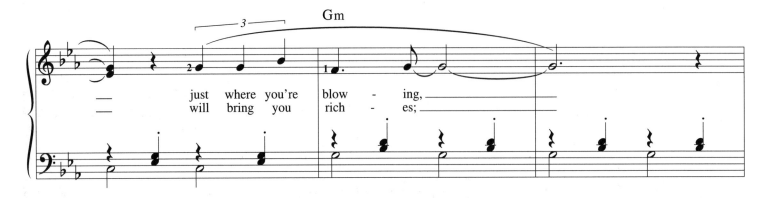

just where you're blow-ing,
will bring you rich-es;

THE DAY WE FIND LOVE

Words & Music by Eliot Kennedy & Helen Boulding

AROUND THE WORLD

Words & Music by Mortimer, Harvey, Rowebottom & Stannard

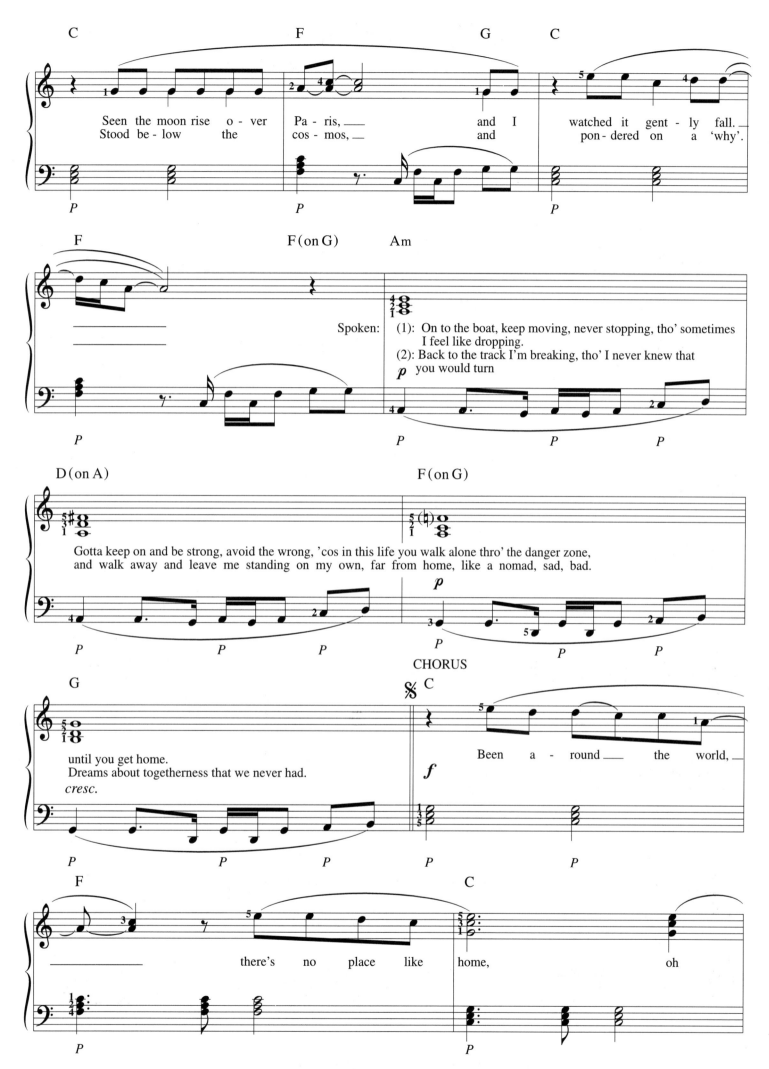

CALL THE MAN

Words & Music by Andy Hill & Peter Sinfield

YOU MUST LOVE ME

Music by Andrew Lloyd Webber
Lyrics by Tim Rice

DISCO 2000

Music by Pulp
Lyrics by Jarvis Cocker

LOVE SHINE A LIGHT

Words & Music by Kimberley Rew

I BELIEVE I CAN FLY

Words & Music by Robert Kelly

GIRLS AND BOYS

Words & Music by Damon Albarn, Graham Coxon, Alex James & David Rowntree

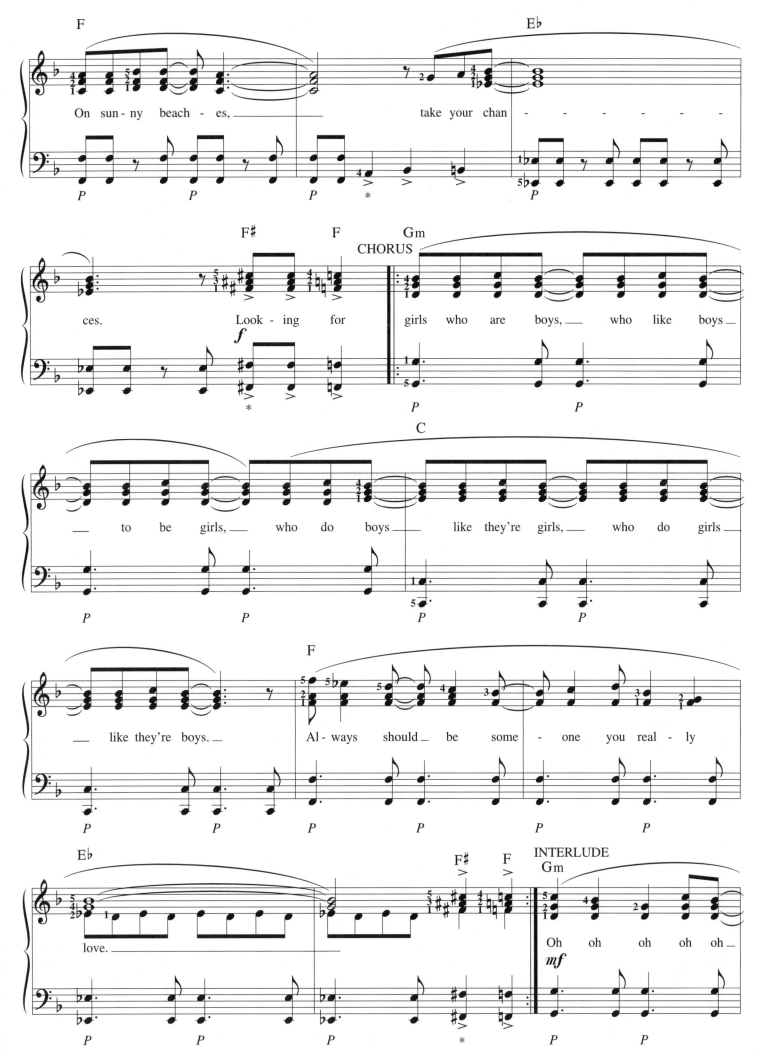

TIME TO SAY GOODBYE

Words & Music by F. Sartori & L. Quarantotto
Adapted by Frank Peterson

SPICE UP YOUR LIFE

Words & Music by Geri Halliwell, Emma Bunton, Melanie Brown, Melanie Chisholm,
Victoria Aadams, Richard Stannard & Matt Rowe